24 MAZES

HEN FR
R IED
Y

LABORATORY
BOOKS
ASTORIA, QUEENS

Laboratory Books LLC
35-19 31st Avenue, No. 4R
Astoria, NY 11106
www.laboratorybooks.xyz

First edition
10 9 8 7 6 5 4 3 2 1

ISBN 978-1-946053-04-6

Library of Congress Control Number:
2017942384

Heads set in Industry Inc
Text set in Factoria

Printed in the Czech Republic

CONTENTS

INTRODUCTION

I worked on the mazes in this book slowly, over the course of a dozen years. Some went through several versions before I thought they looked right. (Often I could visualize a maze quite clearly but had trouble figuring out how to draw it.) I wanted the whole series of twenty-four mazes to have the greatest possible variety, in order to demonstrate the versatility of mazes as an art form.

A two-dimensional maze functions as both a picture and a puzzle. What's more, its puzzle aspect can be just as expressive as its picture aspect. By modifying the nature of the paths (how they are defined, how often they twist or turn, whether they cross over each other) and the intersections (how often they occur, how many branches they have), the maze designer can produce countless different sensations of movement. In the best mazes, the picture aspect and the puzzle aspect reinforce each other, creating an aesthetic experience that a picture or a puzzle alone could not. (Life-size three-dimensional mazes, like hedge mazes and corn mazes, have their own aesthetic criteria.)

While most of the mazes developed organically, I also tried to address some specific artistic questions, such as the tension between illusionistic space and the flatness of the picture (or maze) plane; the abstraction of natural forms; and the construction of complex forms from simple elements. These are hardly new areas of inquiry, but I hope the interplay between picture and maze will provide a fresh way of looking at them.

I drew the mazes at the size you see them here, on ordinary typing paper, with Pigma Micron pens over a pencil underdrawing. My indispensable tools for the under-drawings were Schaedler Precision Rules and a mechanical pencil that took 0.3 millimeter leads.

I used a computer to calculate certain shapes, such as the cate-naries (curves formed by hanging chains or ropes) in maze 9, and I used random numbers to generate certain patterns, such as the crin-kles in maze 14. In general, though, I used only the most rudimentary geometry and algebra, and I never hesitated to fudge the numbers for the sake of art.

There are written instructions opposite each maze, along with an illustration showing how to follow the paths, or how the paths branch at an intersection. (However, this illustration should not be taken as a hint to the solution.)

At the back of the book, I have also included a brief tutorial on maze design. As with any art or craft, the more you know about how it's done, the better you can appre-ciate (or criticize) it.

1. AN ORDINARY MAZE

There are two dead ends in the lower left-hand corner. Find your way from one to the other.

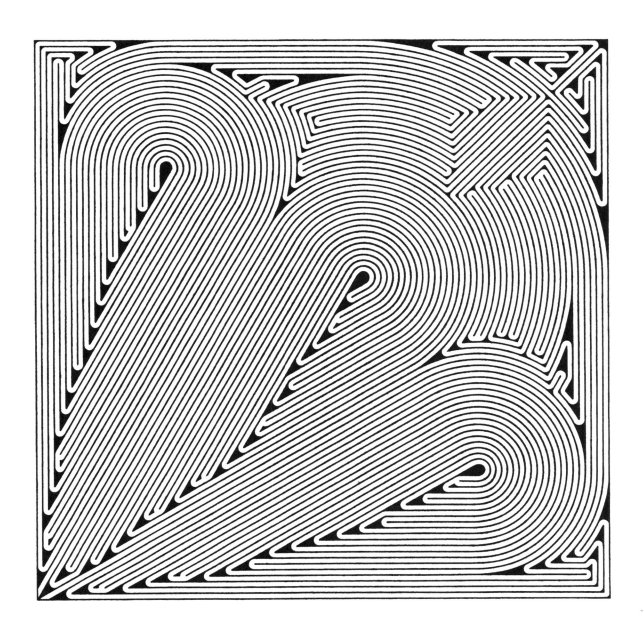

2. THICK AND THIN

Find your way from the T of THICK to the N of THIN, or vice versa. You will have to travel between the lines in some places and on the lines in others, switching methods when you turn at an intersection.

3. TRAMP ART

Find your way from the blank triangle at bottom left to the one at top right, or vice versa.

4. PHANTOM TRIANGLES

Find your way from one large white triangle to the other, passing only through the narrow gaps at the corners of the small white triangles.

5. RATTAN

Find your way from one
black dot to the other.

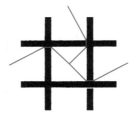

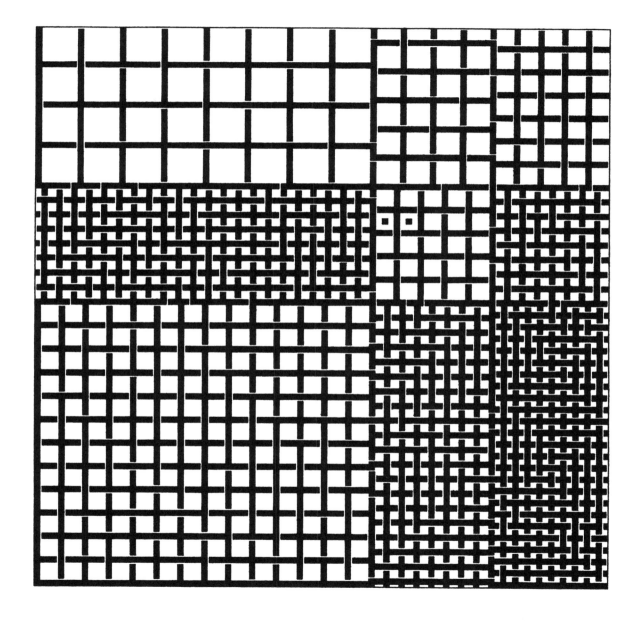

6. DISTRICTS

Leave the center through one gap and return through the other.

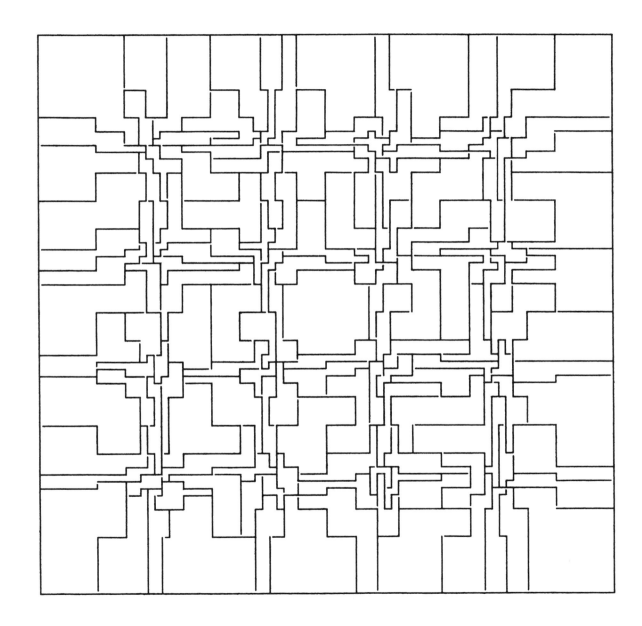

7. WHIRLPOOLS

Find your way from one star to the other.

8. COSMATESQUE

There are two round spirals close to the center of the maze. Find your way from one to the other.

9. CATENARIES

Find your way from one loose
end to the other, following
the hanging ropes as they
pass over and under each
other. There is one dead end
in each spool.

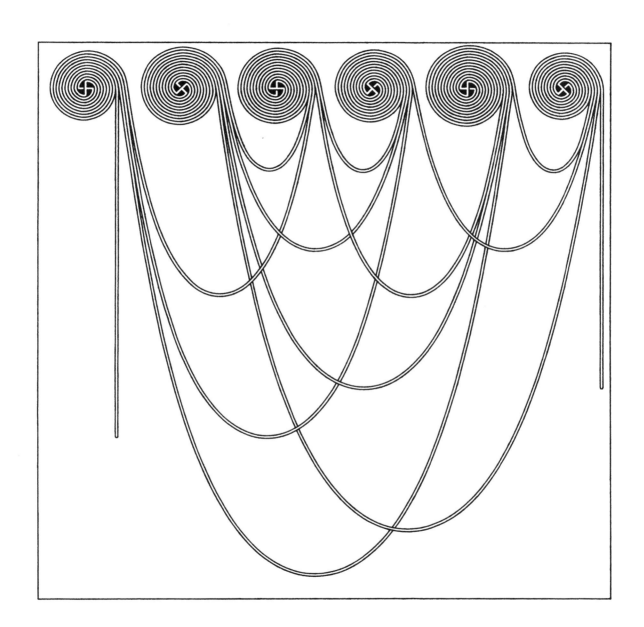

10. ARCHIMEDEAN SPIRAL

Find your way from the space at center to the space at top right.

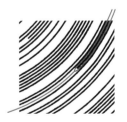

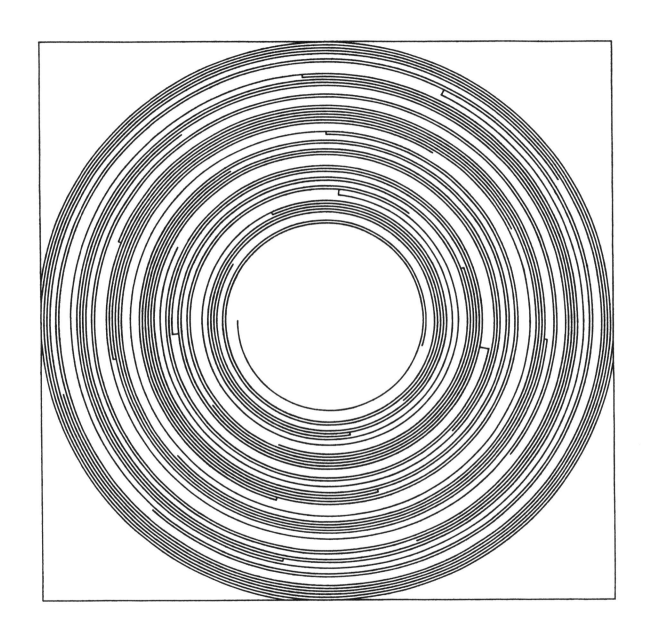

11. LOGARITHMIC SPIRAL

The rays emanate from twenty-one nodes. Find your way from the node at the right edge to the one closest to the center, or vice versa. Travel along the rays as they pass over and under each other, and move from one ray to another where they merge.

12. GRAVITY

Leave the center by one passage and return by the other.

13. WILMURT

Find your way from Earth's western hemisphere to its eastern one, or vice versa.

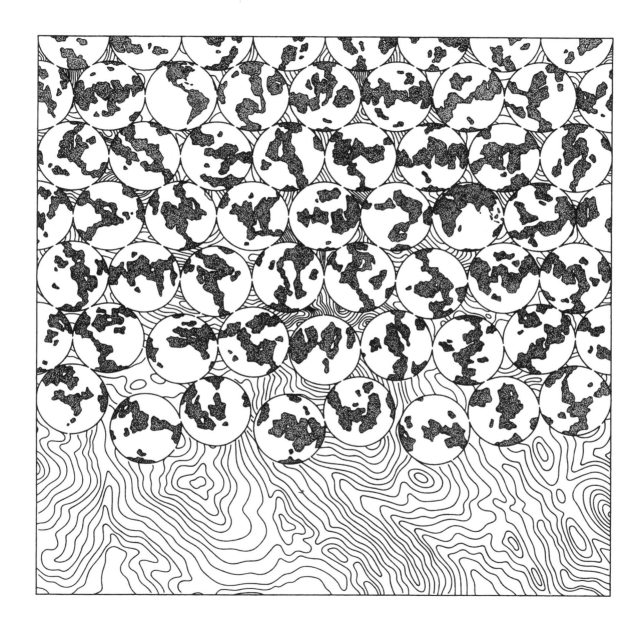

14. LANDSCAPE WITH ORBS

Leave the top-right orb by one passage and return by another.

15. TREES

There are two pears on the middle tree. Find your way from one to the other, following the paths as they cross over and under each other.

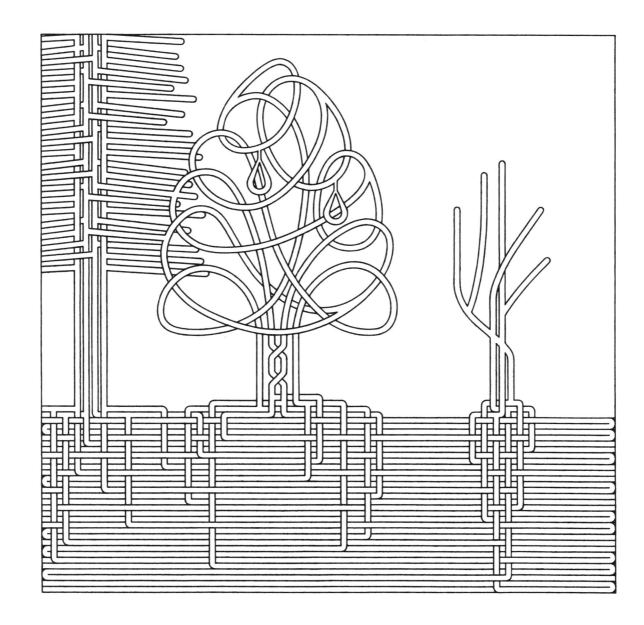

16. CITY

There are two loose ends
sticking out of the ground.
Find your way from one to
the other. Paths can cross
over and under each other
above ground, but not below
ground.

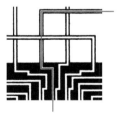

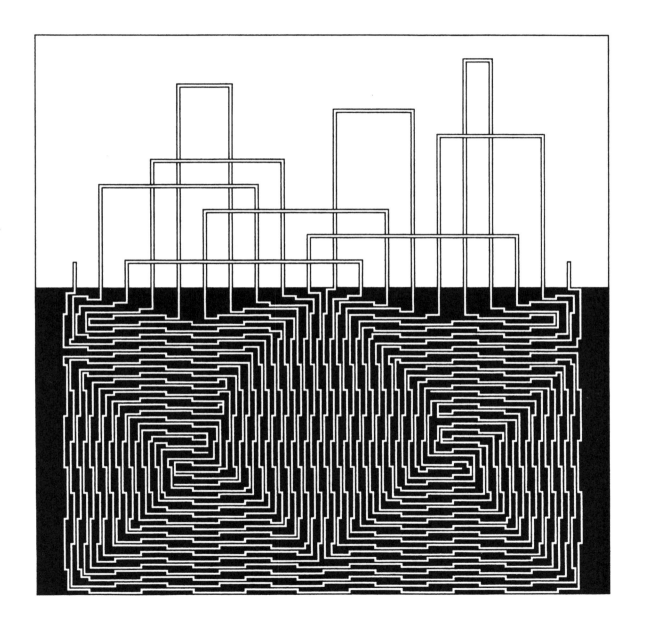

17. ZEBRA

Find your way from one white dot to the other, ignoring the changes in color.

18. THE BIRDS AND THE BEES

Find your way from one beak to the other.

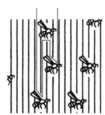

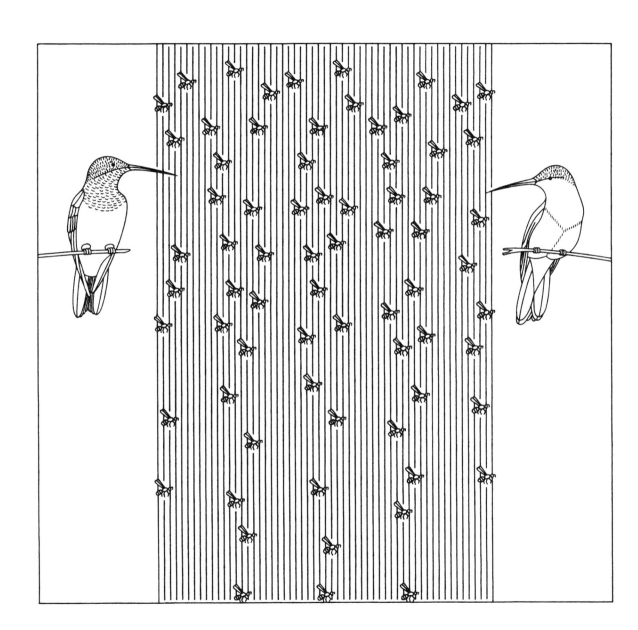

19. ROCK GARDEN

Find your way from the large rock at bottom left to those at top, or vice versa.

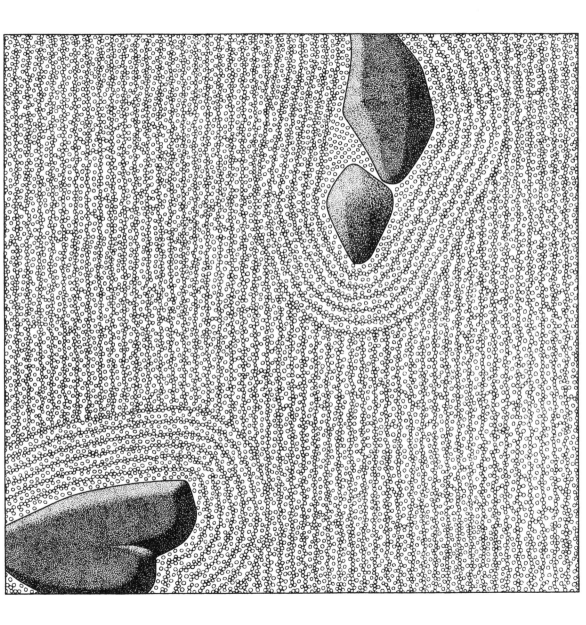

20. BLOCKS

Enter bottom left and exit top
right, or vice versa.

21. MAZE MAZE MAZE

Find your way from the bottom M at bottom left to the top E at top right, or vice versa. (There are four layers of words.) The paths cross over and under each other.

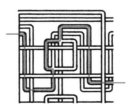

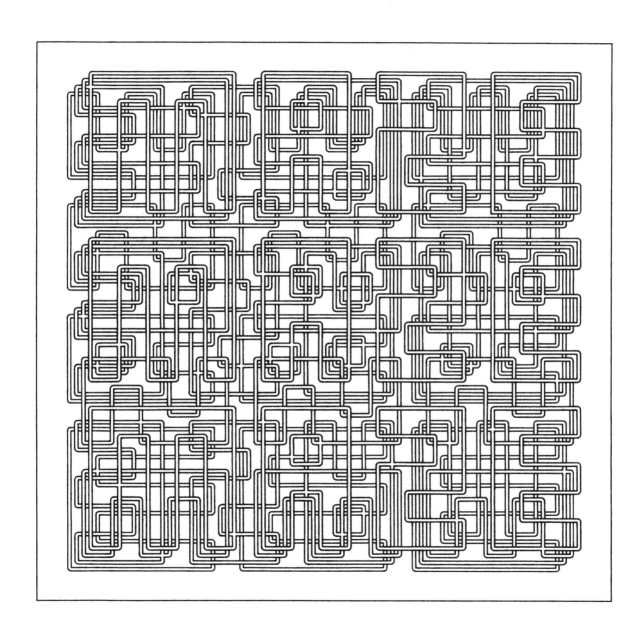

22. CHORDS

Find your way from one loose end to the other, following the strings as they pass over and under each other. The knots are three-way intersections.

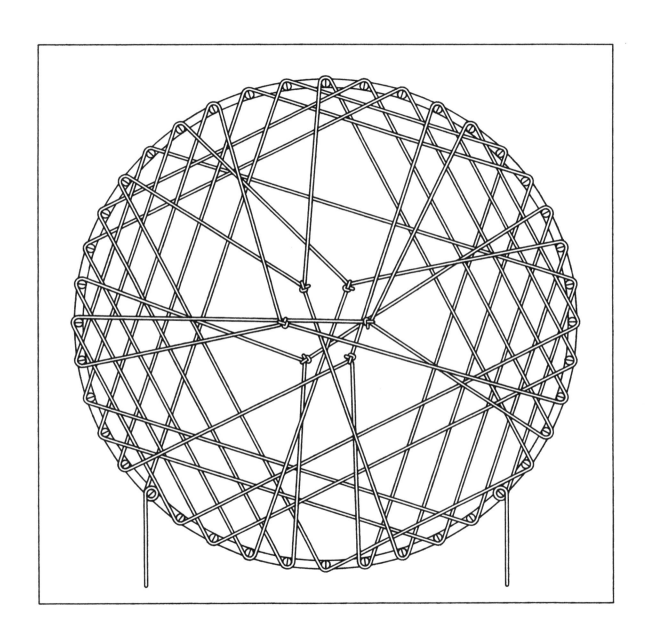

23. TWO-POINT PERSPECTIVE

Find your way from one
white dot to the other, traveling along the black.

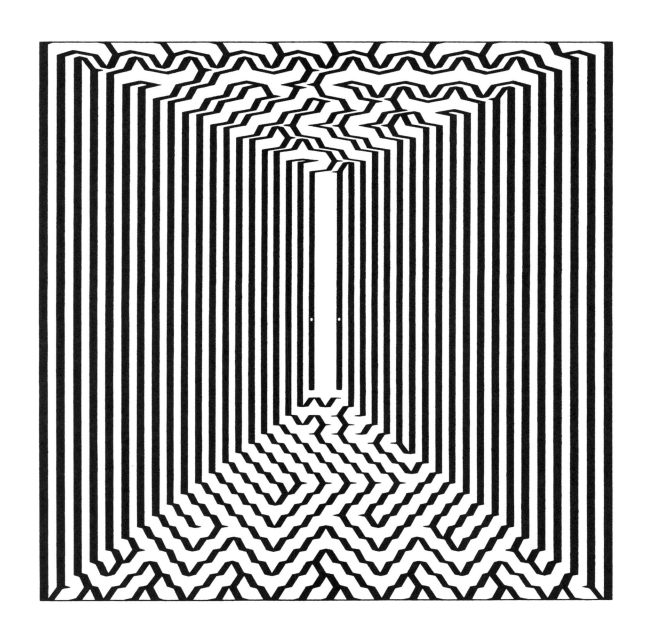

24. SHUTTERS

Find your way from the dead
end at bottom left to the one
at top right, or vice versa.
Follow along the paths as if
the maze were not cut apart.

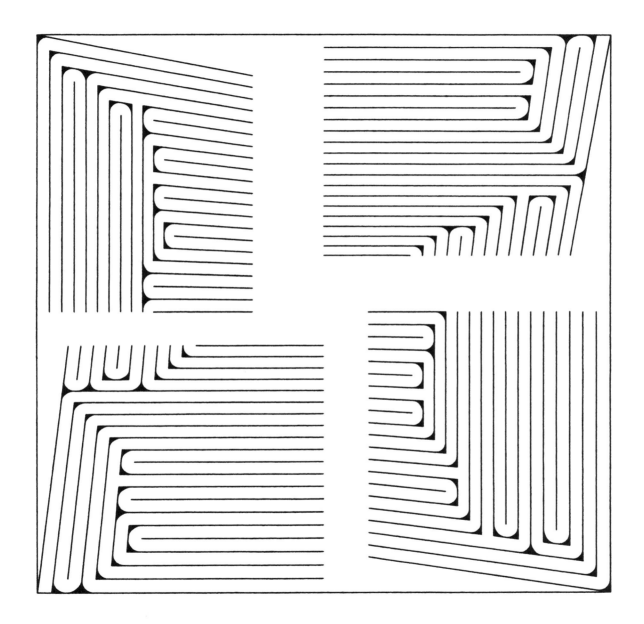

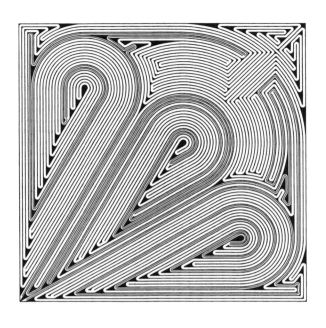

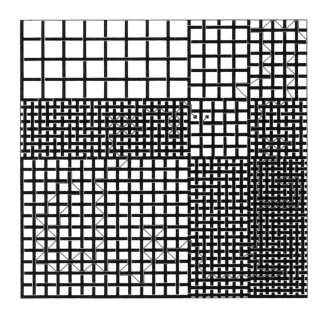
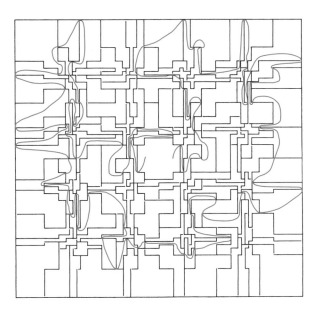
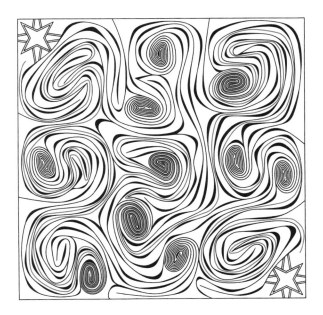

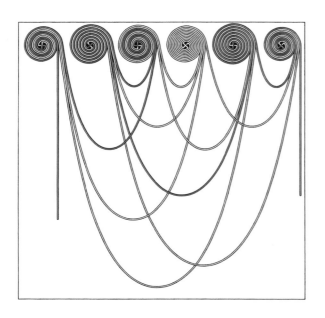
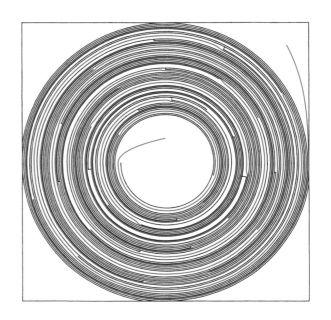

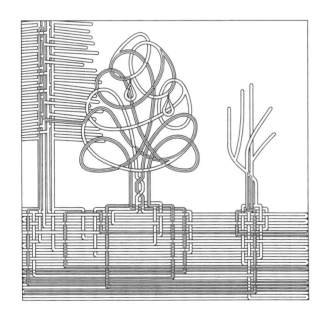

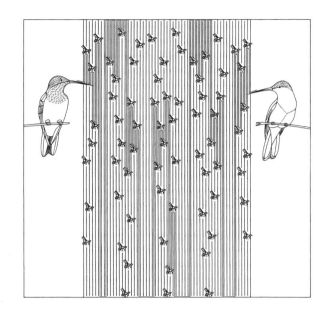

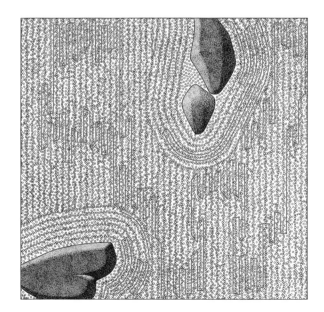

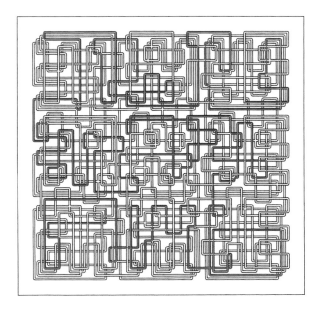
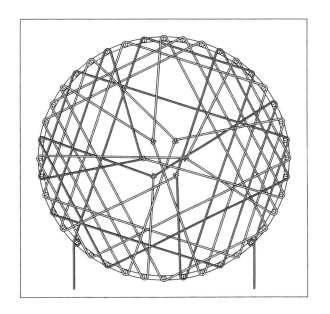
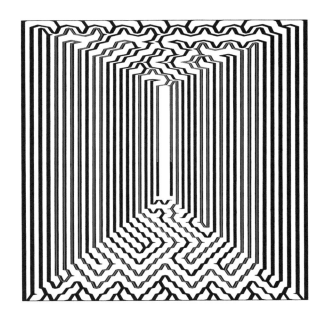
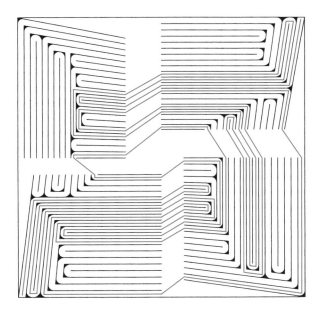

DESIGNING A MAZE

Let's start with a path from one point to another. This is the backbone of our maze.

Next let's decide how many wrong turns our maze will have.

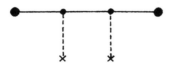

Of course, each intersection can lead to more than one dead end.

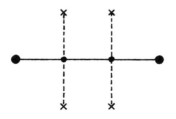

And, if we prefer, we can turn our dead ends into endless loops.

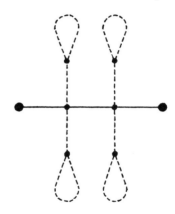

In this schematic form, our maze is very easy. In order to turn it into a real puzzle, we'll need to represent it in a form too complicated for the eye to take in all at once.

One way to do that is to make the paths long and twisty. We can make them zigzag—or spiral.

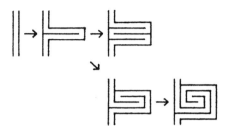

And we can make them do those things together.

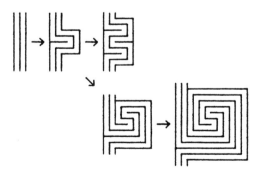

We'll also need to pay attention to the position and shape of the intersections in the maze. For example, if you were traveling from left to right and came to this intersection, would you choose path A or B? What if you thought I was trying to trick you?

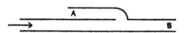

With these ideas in mind, let's try turning the second figure on the opposite page—the one with just two dead ends—into a proper maze. To keep ourselves organized, we'll build the maze on a grid of a predetermined size—say, twelve by twelve squares. (That's just for this exercise; ordinarily I'd use a larger grid.)

Here's one possible design. In this one, it's harder to find your way from bottom left to top right than vice versa, because of the position and shape of the intersections. (Maybe that's okay, as long as we tell people to start at the bottom left.)

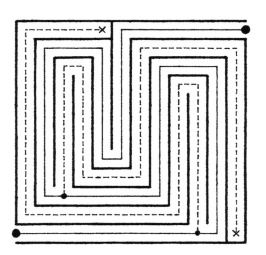

Here's another possible design, which should be of more or less equal difficulty in both directions.

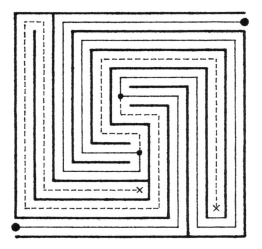

Let's say we're satisfied with the basic design of the maze for now. However, it's still rather plain-looking.

We can make it more attractive,
and more of a puzzle, by distorting
or disguising the grid. Here are two
possibilities.

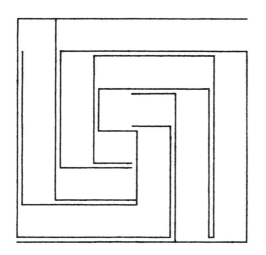

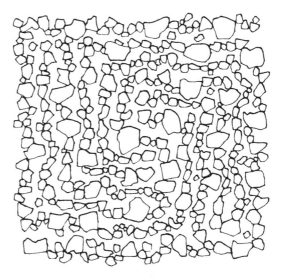

At this point, maybe we should go
back and ask ourselves what some
of the faults of our example maze
are. How could we fix them by
using a larger grid, or using the
existing grid more cleverly?

Or should we use a grid at all?